T0197197

THE EMPATH DETOX
11 Days, 11 Ways to Raise Your Vibration

C O L L E E N   W O L A K

BALBOA.PRESS
A DIVISION OF HAY HOUSE

Balboa Press books may be ordered through booksellers or by contacting:

Balboa Press
A Division of Hay House
1663 Liberty Drive
Bloomington, IN 47403
www.balboapress.com
844-682-1282

Print information available on the last page.

ISBN: 979-8-7652-3457-0 (sc)
ISBN: 979-8-7652-3458-7 (e)

Balboa Press rev. date: 04/06/2023

CONTENTS

INTRODUCTION

❝

To make the impact you are meant
to make in this world, it's imperative
that you are living in your highest
vibration possible.

As empaths, our ability to feel energy is what allows us to connect to others, understand what they're going through, and alter how we show up in the world for their sake and for ourselves. Oftentimes, it's also what prevents us from living in our highest vibration, as our energy becomes susceptible to the rapid shifts in energy around us – and more importantly, the effect those shifts have on our own emotions.

It's a frequent occurrence that I walk into a crowded space and unapologetically declare, "I can't stay here." When I'm in a place where the collective energy is in direct contradiction to mine, I can become so overwhelmed that I feel the need to physically leave, unless there is a secluded space that provides me a big enough "bubble" for protection.

The energy of other people and our surroundings plays a profound role in our own vibration. As an empath, you are highly vulnerable to the energy of everything around you, both positive and negative.

What does it mean to be in a "high vibration"?

Contrary to popular belief, it doesn't mean that you are happy at all times. It simply means that you are in alignment with what feels authentic and good to you, and the life you want to live. You feel empowered that what you're allowing into your life matches up with where you want to be and what you want to move towards..

High vibe situations might include:

- Being in a relationship that makes you feel seen and loved, with someone you respect and love in return

- Having a career that feels purpose-driven, surrounded by leaders you respect, and coworkers who feel like teammates

- Surrounding yourself with friends you can be yourself around. The friends you would call first if you lost your job or broke up with your partner. The ones who've probably seen you naked or at your most vulnerable. The ones who've held your hair back after a ratchet night out. *Those* friends.

Most activities, in and of themselves, aren't specifically "high vibe" or "low vibe."

A night of drinking with friends can be high vibe if you're all in good spirits and having a great time. Now, if we throw in a few rounds of shots and some people you aren't too fond of, you've got the makings of an instant energy shift.

By contrast, imagine being alone in your living room, trying to drink away your sadness. Same physical activity, much different circumstances - *and much different vibe.*

One could easily come up with activities that seem obviously dark or low vibe: excessive drinking, partaking in drugs, cheating on a partner, stealing, and so on. But there are much more innocent things we do day in and day out that don't feel authentic to us or the life we want to lead.

If you're feeling consistent anxiety or stress about a person or situation, it's worth diving into what about it doesn't feel good to you, and making any necessary adjustments.

Make it your *job* to find peace in your inner world and you'll never be in lower vibrations for too long.

So how do we keep our vibration high and unaffected?

The "easiest" thing in the world would be to simply remove ourselves from situations, people and places that don't make us feel at peace. But of course, this is unrealistic in practice and contrary to our missions here in this time and place. You are an empath for a reason. Your sensitivities are your superpower, And the people of the world, in all vibrational states, need you.

Our best defense - and ultimately our best *offense* - is to do everything in our power to raise and maintain our own vibration. When we are not protecting our energy, we create space for lower frequencies to enter in, blocking us from all that we are here to create and do. The intent of this book is to provide my fellow sensitive souls with the tools to raise and maintain a high vibration.

While I don't particularly like gimmicks ("30 Days to Enlightenment!"), I wanted to provide an experience that would feel tangible and *not* overwhelming, for perhaps already overwhelmed, empathic souls.

Tackle one item per day over eleven days, spread it out over several weeks, or implement multiple tactics all at once. Find the strategy that works for you and your life. You can't mess this up!

CLEAR OTHERS' ENERGY
From Your Space

❝
Only love, light, and positivity are
welcome in this space.

The energy of those around us doesn't only affect us when they're physically in our presence. Their energy can linger for hours or longer, in both our aura and our physical space. What's more, we often don't even need to be in the *presence* of our close friends and family members in order to feel their emotions.

When I am feeling heavy or down for seemingly no reason, I will stop to ask myself if the emotions I'm feeling are actually mine. Oftentimes, they're not. When you have close bonds with others, it's common to have energetic cords running between you. The best thing you can do to protect and maintain a high vibration is to consistently clear out any heavy or lower energy.

There are a number of ways to quickly shift your vibration and transmute any stale or stagnant energy from your space.

Let the Light In

In daylight hours, open the curtains and a few windows. The light and fresh air will instantly brighten the energy, leaving your space feeling less heavy.

Burn Sage (Smudging)

In addition to providing many medicinal benefits in its natural state, burning sage is thought to help ward off any lower energies that may be lingering in your physical space.

Before you begin, you'll definitely want to open a window or door - afterall, any lower energy needs a way to "get out"! Light the sage, and let it burn for a few moments before blowing out the flame. You should now be seeing smoke, which you will slowly guide throughout your home.

I find it helpful to set an intention for the smudging by repeating a short mantra out loud or in my head as I smudge. My favorite mantra: "Only love, light and positivity are welcome in this space."

For extra credit, sage yourself by waving the sage stick around your body. Just ignore any strange looks from your spouse, roommate or pets. Perhaps wave it over them as well :)

Light Some Incense

Similar to sage, incense can help break up dense energy in your space and purify the air. While any scent will serve this purpose, here are a few of my favorites for clearing my home:

- **Frankincense:** Favored for its ability to ward off negative energies, it's a known stress reducer. It's also known to enhance clairvoyance, making it a great meditation tool as well.

- **Sandalwood:** In addition to offering protection, it reduces irritability and aggressiveness - *making it a great scent to use after a fight with a friend or loved one!*

- **Patchouli:** While many are not a fan of the strong scent of patchouli, it's known to powerfully clear out negativity and invoke positivity.

Protect Your Energy with Crystals

Crystals are a wonderful tool, both for increasing your own energy and providing protection against *other* energies. A few great crystals for protecting your energy:

- **Black Tourmaline** acts as a protective shield, preventing others from projecting their energy onto you. In addition to carrying this stone with you, you may want to place it near the entrance to your home for added protection.

- **Pyrite**, commonly referred to as "Fools Gold", has a reflective quality which helps to deflect negative influences surrounding you. It's also believed to boost confidence and help with making important decisions.

For this reason, many consider it to also be a stone of wealth and abundance.

- **Black Kyanite** works to block any negative or toxic energy, transmuting it instead into an energy of love and light. In other words, you're not only pushing negative energy away, but also sending it back into the world as clean, positive energy so that others will not be affected by it either.

Simply Ask Your Guides

If you believe in and feel connected to your spirit guides, you can vocally set an intention with them to clear your mind, body, and physical space of any lingering lower vibe energy. A simple request could be, "Please protect me from any energies that do not serve my highest good."

Recap

Energy Clearing Tools

- Let the light in *(curtains and windows)*
- Burn sage
- Light incense *(Frankincense, Sandalwood, Patchouli)*
- Protect your energy with crystals *(Black Tourmaline Pyrite, Black Kyanite)*
- Simply ask your guides
- Set an intention of clearing your space
- Create an energetic aura around yourself
- Fill your space with music
- Shower meditation

**Don't have any of the above items on hand? Try one
or more of the following:**

1. Light a candle and set an intention of clearing your
   space. Say aloud, "Only positivity, love, and light are
   welcome in this space."

2. Create an energetic aura around you. As you enter a
   space in which you anticipate chaotic energy, picture
   yourself enveloped in a white, cloud-like bubble that
   wards off negative energy, but still allows energy to
   flow outward from you.

3. Fill your space with music. Visit my website, <u>www.
   justonewoo.com</u>, for a link to my recommended
   playlist for clearing out negative energy.

4. Do a shower meditation. As you exhale, visualize
   the water washing away any negativity you have
   physically accumulated over the course of the day.

Additional Journaling

What thoughts or feelings does this chapter bring up for you?

_____

_____

_____

_____

_____

_____

_____

_____

_____

_____

_____

_____

_____

_____

_____

_____

_____

_____

_____

_____

_____

_____

_____

CONSIDER CHANGING YOUR RELATIONSHIP
with Social Media

> "
> Be connected where you need
> and want to be connected, while
> maintaining boundaries to protect
> your energy.

Having spent the majority of my professional career in marketing, which is of course heavily centered these days around social media, I feel almost disloyal saying that I feel social media is having a disastrous effect on our collective vibration. Social media can connect and unite us in so many wonderful ways, while also creating a gaping divide in other ways. As an empath, you may feel those downsides of social platforms in heavier ways than most.

Personally speaking, there's not much on social media that, on a surface level, triggers me in a specific way. It is instead the ***heart*** of the content – the intent and the emotions that I feel from the person posting – that most often affects my energy, and seldomly in a good way.

As empaths, we often get small pings of energy from things around us, and social media feeds are no exception. If you are engaging with social media content for a significant amount of time each day, those individual pings are likely throwing a snowball of energy at your vibration.

There are two big reasons for this:

1. You are picking up on the energy behind others' posts, whether those posts have anything to do with you or not.
2. There will be things shared on social media that do in fact have *everything* to do with you - whether it is the poster's intention or something you are internalizing on your own.

I speak and write a lot about triggers - words and situations that stir up emotion within us as they hit on our biggest pain points or insecurities. In theory, if we have a level of knowing that that's what's happening, we should be able to stop these triggers in their tracks. In practice, it's a little more difficult, especially for those of us who "think" with our emotions, in addition to simple logic or pragmatism.

What's worse is that we're often getting triggered by things that aren't even real… alter ego lives people put out for all to see.

How often do you see a photo of a stunningly happy couple with a note about how magical their love is, only to hear weeks later that the happy couple is now parting ways? We show the world what we want and need them to see.

While it may be true that you're in Paris having the time of your life, people won't likely know the full truth of the situation – that you maxed out your credit card to get there, that you're wishing you had someone to share the experience with, or that you made seven attempts at getting that perfect social media pic.

While holding space for all of the wonderful things about social media, we can also acknowledge the detrimental effects, including additional division, and feelings of confusion, emptiness, or loneliness.

I'm most concerned about the impact on young children and teenagers, as they compare themselves to their peers or see what fun they're missing out on. If we're not careful and conscious users of social platforms, they have the power to negatively impact our entire collective vibration.

So what's the solution?

Do we just remove social media from our existence? Of course not. As empaths, it's our job to manage and master our energies, not simply hide from them. But perhaps we can limit the amount of time we put ourselves in situations that we know so easily impact us. By doing so, our energy is better prepared to handle the *unavoidable* triggers and pings we will encounter throughout the day.

There are a number of ways to manage your social media experience in a way that allows you to be connected where you need and want to be, while also providing boundaries to protect your mental and emotional health.

Consider reducing your time spent on social platforms

Try limiting yourself to just a few minutes each day, rather than allowing it to be your go-to activity when you have a few spare moments - sitting at a red light or waiting in a line at the grocery store - or as a backdrop activity when you're watching tv.

You might need to get pretty specific in setting this boundary to make it stick. Perhaps you allow for 5 minutes in the morning and 5 minutes in the evening for social media scrolling. The idea here is to get used to it being a more conscious activity versus a way to pass the time.

Take a close look at who you're following

A good start to limiting your exposure to potential triggers would be filtering through your friend and follower lists and weeding out people who aren't actually in your circle. It may be fun having an easy, authorized way to spy on your high school crush, but is that really necessary?

If you haven't spoken to someone *in person* or *on the phone* in the last year or more, with perhaps the exclusion of extended family members, there may not be a valid case to stay connected on social media. If they're not triggering you, then no problem. But if their content affects you in any way but *good*, they've gotta go.

For those you are connected to in "real life" whose posts negatively affect your energy, you could simply unfollow them versus removing them. This way, you won't hurt anyone's feelings, yet they won't appear in your feed.

Filter your feed to only show posts from specific people

A filtered feed can provide a more peaceful social media experience, allowing you the benefit of the awesome aspects of social media, while mostly removing the negative. You could also consider an aggregator app, which allows you to curate your feeds, seeing only the content that matters most to you. *Visit my website, www.justonewoo.com, for an updated list of aggregator apps.*

Recap

Managing Your Social Media Experience

- Limit your time on social platforms
- Unfollow people you have no connection to or interest in
- Mute or unfollow people whose activity triggers you
- Use an aggregator app to curate your feed experience

Challenge

Social Media Decluttering

Spend 20 minutes doing the following:

- Unfriend / unfollow anyone you no longer care to be connected to. If their content isn't interesting to you, and you don't care if they know what you're up to, get rid of 'em.
- In your feed settings, hide posts from people whose content triggers you. This is a softer alternative to unfollowing their account entirely.

Additional Journaling

What thoughts or feelings does this chapter bring up for you?

_____

_____

_____

_____

_____

_____

_____

_____

_____

_____

_____

_____

_____

_____

_____

_____

_____

_____

_____

LIMIT ALCOHOL
Consumption

❝

As we drink, we often experience an immediate shift to our vibration, as well as that of others around us.

Okay. Let's talk about *drinks.*

Not surprisingly, alcohol has a significant impact on our energy, and that can take us in several different directions.

A few glasses of wine might put you in a peaceful and meditative space. For most people, though, there is a tipping point, where we go from relaxed and chill to paranoid, neurotic, belligerent, and perhaps worse.

I was never drawn to alcohol growing up. I'm almost positive I was beyond the legal drinking age when I had my first real sip – Fuzzy Navel Boone's Farm, which in fact, might not actually qualify as a real sip.

In high school, I had a small circle of close friends, who, like me, were not ruling the party scene. It's not that I was specifically "anti-alcohol" – I just literally didn't have access to it or a reason to think there was anything special about it. In college, I was very overweight and a bit of a loner, and quite frankly, 2am Waffle House nightcaps with my roommates were more my style ("smothered and covered").

These days, I would 100% classify myself as a social drinker. If I'm not being social, I'm likely not drinking. The problem with that comes when I become *really* social. If I'm in a phase where I'm out socializing 4-5 nights a week, it's quite possible that I'll have 10-20 drinks in a week. Minimum. That's not only a lot of empty calories, it's also a lot of extra money and can have a huge impact on productivity and emotional wellbeing.

There are certain friend circles and activities that almost always include drinks, and for the duration of our time together. There is much fun that can be had in that - a break down of walls, lots of openness, and a feeling of release. But there is a lot of drama that can come with that as well.

As we drink, we experience a shift to our vibration, as well as that of others around us. As empaths, we are going to be *extra* sensitive, not only to the alcohol we are taking in, but to the mood changes in ourselves, our friends, and even strangers in our immediate vicinity.

And let's not forget about your quality of sleep. After a night of heavy drinking, you may notice that you wake up more frequently in the middle of the night. The alcohol is interrupting your REM cycle - i.e. deep sleep. This is just one of the *many* reasons you may feel sluggish after an extreme night out.

Having said that, I'm not one to recommend or adhere to a "this or that" life. As is the case with social media, there are a number of boundaries we can put into place that allow us our freedom, while also protecting our energy.

Evaluate your friend circle

Do you have friends that you simply *have* to drink with in order to want to be around them? Or with whom you feel uncomfortable or awkward around without the safety net of a beer or vodka soda? If that's the case, it might be time to evaluate whether those relationships actually contribute anything meaningful to your life.

Introduce new non-drinking activities to your circle

It's possible that you and your crew are just unimaginative when it comes to social outings. Meeting up at a local bar may have become your easy default. Try switching up your gatherings to include activities less centered around alcohol. I'm not suggesting that everyone needs to stop drinking, but perhaps you get out of the "local bar rut" you have settled into. Trying a new restaurant could bring something new to the table that removes the focus from alcohol, even if you *do* have a drink or two.

Get mindful about your drinking

It's easy to match others drink-for-drink when we're out, ordering one for every round that everyone else is having. Perhaps you could slow-sip your drinks, or alternate a non-alcoholic drink such as a club soda with lime with your alcoholic drinks. At some point, you're going to get to a place of diminishing returns anyways.

When you're mindful of your tipping point, you can relax and enjoy yourself, while also knowing you won't have any drama, your vibe will stay high, and you won't feel miserable the next morning. Win–win–win.

Know that it's possible to be in a drinking environment and not drink

This can be tough, but if you have a warm, authentic friend circle, it won't be an issue to spend time with them and not drink. It's important to note that regardless of your drinking status, you're going to take in the vibrational shifts in others around you, which could still leave you feeling heavy. Just be mindful of those feelings, and get comfortable bailing out of the festivities when you've had enough.

I'd like to make one more case for cutting or limiting your alcohol intake. As an empath, you are here to serve a higher purpose. You're a natural teacher and healer, and that is the beauty of this gift. If you have a nagging feeling that you are drinking "too much" or that it's holding you back from what you're meant to be creating and doing, that's likely your higher self trying to get through to you. It may be worth taking stock of your current situation and seeing how you can reduce that impact on your life.

Even 3–4 days in a row of not drinking can help give you some clarity on that, as you'll notice the difference in what your days look like - your level of productivity, your energy, your mood and so on.

For anyone triggered that I'm not making a bigger case for completely cutting out alcohol, let me add this:

People who strongly connect with being on a spiritual path – particularly those who identify as "Indigos" – are not traditionally great rule followers. It's not in our nature to simply do or think as we're told without question, or to live a black-and-white, this-or-that life. We often exist somewhere in the middle, in the *gray* – and that is where we thrive.

The biggest win of all would be to create a lifestyle that allows us to seamlessly incorporate all of the things we love into a highly vibrational way of living. If you feel like having a glass of wine, you'll have a glass of wine. If you feel like having four drinks at a party, you'll have four drinks at a party. But you'll also have the discernment to know what that might mean for your energy at that time, and in the day(s) following, and adjust your life accordingly.

There's no room for fear, shame, blame, or guilt in a high vibe life, so let's remove that from the equation.

If this chapter resonated with you and you feel like alcohol may be impacting your life in some way, I would offer a recommendation to consider where you can shift when it comes to drinking.

Recap

Managing Your Relationship with Alcohol

- Evaluate your friend circle
- Introduce new non-drinking activities to your circle
- Get mindful about your drinking
- Know that it's possible to be in a drinking environment and not drink

Challenge

Drinking Mindfulness

Complete the questions below. Consider how each question makes you feel, and what it brings up for you. You may want to take advantage of the notes section to dive in deeper.

1. How many alcoholic drinks do you estimate you had last week?

2. Of those, how many felt:
   Celebratory / Mindful: _____
   Automatic: _____

3. Of the "automatic" drinks, were there any common denominators?

People: _____

Location: _____

Mood: _____

4. Do you feel that an adjustment to your relationship is necessary? Yes_____ No_____

5. If you answered "yes" above, list one change you'd like to make when it comes to alcohol:

_____

_____

_____

_____

_____

_____

_____

6. Why do you want to make this change?

_____

_____

_____

_____

_____

_____

_____

Additional Journaling

What thoughts or feelings does this chapter bring up for you?

_____

_____

_____

_____

_____

_____

_____

_____

_____

_____

_____

_____

_____

_____

_____

_____

_____

_____

_____

_____

ASSESS YOUR
Circle

> " "
> What matters more than who's in
> your circle and how they behave is
> who and how you are when you're
> around them.

There is a commonly referenced idea that we are the average of the five people we spend the most time with.

While you likely have a very diverse group of friends, family members, and others around you, your tightest circle is the best indicator of:

- What your overall vibration will be;

- The activities you will participate in; and

- How you will ultimately live your day-to-day life.

As an empath, you have an especially heightened sensitivity to the energy of others around you, making it even more important to investigate your circle and make changes when necessary.

Understandably, you'll want to surround yourself with the people you love most, regardless of their energy, making it extra important to protect your energy where you can.

It's worth taking a deep dive into what you like most about those in your inner circle and the qualities they possess that add value to your life. You may find that some people need to play a lesser role in your life, while others on the "fringe" of your circle might be worth bringing in more closely.

It should be noted that it's not only who's in your circle and how they behave that's important here. It's about who and how *you* are when you're around them.

Recap

Setting Boundaries With Your Circle

Your tightest circle is the best indicator of:
- What your overall vibration will be
- The activities you will participate in
- How you will ultimately live your day-to-day life

Carefully consider who should be:
- Put in a reduced role
- Edited out completely
- Brought closer into your circle

Challenge

When considering your inner circle, ask yourself:

1. **Who do I spend most of my time with?**

   _____

   _____

   _____

   _____

   _____

2. **Of these individuals:**

   • Who do I enjoy spending time with the most?

   _____

   _____

   _____

   • Whose energy most closely and naturally aligns with mine?

   _____

   _____

   _____

   • Who do I feel most relaxed around?

   _____

   _____

   _____

- Who can sometimes leave me feeling drained?

  _____

  _____

  _____

- What could be changed or shifted to improve this?

  _____

  _____

  _____

3. **Is there anyone I wish I could spend more time with?**

   _____

   _____

   _____

   _____

   _____

- What is preventing that?

  _____

  _____

  _____

As you complete this exercise, notice the answers to the questions above in relation to one another.

For example, if someone you spend the majority of your time with isn't also one of the people you enjoy the most, or is on your list of draining energies, then there may be boundaries that need to be set.

You may even find there are people you need to edit completely out of your life. What is more likely to happen, though, is feeling the need to shift the amount of *time* you spend with certain people, and perhaps the activities you engage in with them. In that case, consider where you can step back to protect your energy, but still have those individuals as key parts of your life.

You may also discover there are people in your world that you feel closely aligned with that you don't see as often as you'd like. It might be time to proactively draw them in closer.

Once you've examined your inner circle, you'll now want to look at the "fringe" - the people you see here and there, but aren't constants in your daily life.

When considering the fringe, ask yourself:

1. Who do I spend time with that I seldom or perhaps never initiate contact with?

    _____

    _____

    _____

    _____

- Follow-up: If they never reached out, would I even think to call or see them?

  _____

  _____

  _____

2. Who do I regret making plans with almost immediately after locking in those plans?

  _____

  _____

  _____

3. Who leaves me feeling low most anytime I see them?

  _____

  _____

  _____

It's safe to say that anyone appearing in the answers to the questions above simply can't play an active role in your high vibrational life. They could be energy vampires - people that drain your energy - who quite possibly don't need to be in your life at all, outside of a casual run-in at a group event.

Why? Because the amount of work you'll have to put in to: preparing your energy prior to seeing them, maintaining it during your time together, and clearing once you part ways just might not be worth it.

Of course, there are people that fit these specs whom we have to see - family members, coworkers, etc. In such cases, consider how you can be around them, but with boundaries to protect your time and energy.

Where I struggle, and I suspect you might as well, is when I have guilt about turning down invitations or not reaching out to certain people. That empathic guilt that we feel - which is often rooted in how we think the other person might be feeling about that - can force us to do things that we just don't want to do.

But know this: You are not doing anyone any favors by hanging onto a relationship that you're not truly invested in. It would be much kinder in the long run to disengage, allowing them the space to find people who are more closely aligned with their energy.

Additional Journaling

What thoughts or feelings does this chapter bring up for you?

_____

_____

_____

_____

_____

_____

_____

_____

_____

_____

_____

_____

_____

_____

_____

_____

_____

_____

_____

EDIT YOUR
Background

❝
Put yourself in more situations that
allow your mind to be a blank canvas.

When you consider all of the background activity we have going on in our lives, it's no wonder our vibe can get foggy or low, not to mention how distracted our mind can become. How can we possibly spend any quality time in thought if the tv or music is always playing in the backdrop?

I only recently discovered how distracted I've become on my daily walks. I almost always have a podcast or music blaring through my headphones... anything to fill the void and occupy my brain for the duration of my walk.

In hindsight, it's no surprise to me that some of my best, most creative ideas have come to me when I've gone walking in nature without my phone. In fact, I dreamt up this book about three minutes into my first non-audio-assisted walk in months. I knew in my gut, the second the idea struck me, that this was something I wanted to explore.

For the next seven days, I went walking with my phone and earbuds, but instead of listening to someone else's thoughts, I voiced my own. Using my phone's voice memo app, I talked through every chapter of this book. Within one week, I had logged more than 50 miles and had a complete books' worth of content on my phone, ready to be transcribed and edited.

Being unattached to external thoughts and words created the space I needed to hear my own, and to weave them into a cohesive narrative.

It's helpful to remember how sensitive we are to others' words, thoughts, and feelings – and that includes others "speaking" to us through a tv, radio, or phone.

Consider what you consistently have playing in the background. Are you consciously and actively wanting to have it on, or is it just filling a void?

Having trouble concentrating on projects?

Switch to instrumental music. Lyrics in music can be distracting to your brain, as is the case with most anything you'd watch on television.

Feeling anxiety or stress?

Change the genre of music to something more calming, or switch the tv from the news to something lighter, perhaps a sitcom.

Having trouble sleeping?

Try listening to binaural beats instead of falling asleep to the tv. A binaural beat is the result of listening to two tones with different frequencies at the same time. This results in a new frequency, which your brain will then work to match. Binaural beat music with a 1-4 Hz frequency is the best for deep, uninterrupted sleep. Visit my website, www.justonewoo.com, for my updated binaural beats playlist faves.

If you *must* fall asleep to the tv, set your tv's sleep timer for 30 minutes to ensure that the sounds from your favorite show are not disrupting you throughout the night.

When we have sound on in the background simply to fill space or "keep us company", we may not be consciously choosing the most beneficial or productive backdrop for our thoughts. Clear the space in your brain for wonderful ideas and inspiration to funnel through. They are already there! We just can't always hear them against the external noise we consistently bring into our world. We are *always* on the brink of great ideas. We just need the space to hear them.

You are an empath for a reason. You have this gift because you're meant to do something amazing with it. If you're unsure about your path and what you're meant to do with your empathic skills, I challenge you to put yourself in more situations that allow your mind to be a blank canvas.

Recap

Creating a High Vibe Background

Try the following:

- For concentration: Switch to instrumental music
- For stress: Prioritize calming music, movies and tv shows
- For sleep: Try binaural beats or setting the tv sleep timer

Challenge

Creating a Blank Canvas for Your Thoughts

- Go on a walk or for a drive with nothing playing in the background at all.
- Record what you spent the most time thinking about and any new ideas or inspiration that came to you.

_____

_____

_____

_____

_____

_____

_____

_____

_____

_____

_____

_____

_____

_____

_____

_____

Additional Journaling

What thoughts or feelings does this chapter bring up for you?

_____

_____

_____

_____

_____

_____

_____

_____

_____

_____

_____

_____

_____

_____

_____

_____

_____

_____

_____

_____

EMBRACE MINDFULNESS & *Meditation*

❝
Create a new relationship with the
thoughts running through your mind.

mind·ful·ness

/ˈmīn(d)f(ə)lnəs/

noun

> a mental state achieved by focusing one's awareness on the present moment, while calmly acknowledging and accepting one's feelings, thoughts, and bodily sensations

The idea of meditation can be tough for many people. And it's no wonder, given how much we naturally multitask in a given day: listening to talk radio while driving, scrolling through social media while watching television, texting while out to dinner. The task of being perfectly still, doing just one thing – which actually requires us to do *no* thing – tends to be a difficult one for most people.

There also seems to be a collective sense that the point of meditation is to completely empty our mind of any thoughts. That had always been my bias, making any attempt to meditate a frustrating one. I always felt that I was doing it wrong, and I just don't have the patience to sit perfectly still and empty. *Or to be wrong.*

The truth is, there is no wrong or right way to meditate, and meditation can take on many forms.

Some of my favorite ways to meditate include:

A few minutes of deep breath work

Before getting out of bed or at any point during the day when your mind needs a reset, try this:

Take a 3-count breath in through the nose, hold for 3 seconds, then a 3-count breath out through the mouth. Repeat for as long as you like or need.

A short walk or run in nature, without background noise from a phone

Consider putting your phone or smart watch on "Do Not Disturb" to prevent interruptions. Simply take in the sights and sounds of nature. You'd be amazed at how much you're missing out on when you walk or run while listening to music!

A guided meditation in bed or in a favorite outdoor spot

You can find a plethora of guided meditations on mobile apps like Calm or Insight Timer, as well as on most streaming services. Still struggling with the "no multitasking" objective? Combining a guided meditation with a walk is great for those who struggle with the need to multitask, allowing you the benefits of a longer meditation while also getting in some fresh air and exercise.

"But what if I can't stop thinking about other things during my meditation?"

A major benefit of meditation is bringing mindfulness to our thoughts. As you begin your meditation practice, it's ok to let your mind wander. Be fully present in your thoughts and take notice of where your mind goes.

As a thought enters your mind, consider how it makes you feel. How is your brain reacting to it? How about your physical body?

Feel free to sit on the thought for a few moments or mentally shoo it away. Imagine in your mind your hand sweeping it off to the side, creating space for either a new thought or a still mind.

The goal is to not get overwhelmed by your thoughts - or the fact that you are having thoughts in the first place. If you're struggling with where your mind is going, bring your awareness back to your breath and the current moment.

Bringing a meditation practice into your life could help you work through the thoughts that are subconsciously always running through your head.

Recap

Simple Ways to Meditate

- Try a few minutes of deep breath work
- Go for a walk or run in nature, without headphones
- Listen to a guided meditation in bed or in a favorite outdoor spot

Challenge

Try a Guided Meditation

- Visit www.justonewoo.com/empathdetox for links to some of my favorite guided meditations. Try one first thing in the morning, before you get out of bed, or before going to sleep.

Additional Journaling

What thoughts or feelings does this chapter bring up for you?

_____

_____

_____

_____

_____

_____

_____

_____

_____

_____

_____

_____

_____

_____

_____

_____

_____

_____

BEGIN A GRATITUDE
Practice

> ❝
> It's nearly impossible to
> simultaneously feel both gratitude
> and despair.

It's incredibly difficult, and perhaps impossible, to simultaneously feel gratitude and be in a low vibration - *try it!* Our thoughts and words set the tone for our own energy as well as the energy around us. When you're feeling low, challenge yourself to rattle off a few things you feel grateful for in your life.

Take it one step further and find something you are grateful for related to the specific situation that has you feeling down.

An example might be the end of a relationship. If you're sad, then there must be positives from that experience that you can look at now with gratitude - otherwise, you wouldn't be feeling so sad. These could range from gratitude for your former partner introducing you to a new set of friends, to gratitude for them giving you a child.

And for a less dramatic example: someone cutting you off in traffic. Could you shift to a place of gratitude that you have a car that allows you the freedom to go anywhere you want to go? Not everyone has that luxury, afterall.

While reactive gratitude can help to quickly shift your energy, a proactive gratitude practice is where it's at for a consistently high vibe life. People who live in gratitude are generally happier, have a deeper sense of empathy for others, experience higher self esteem, and have an increased level of resiliency when hit with life's challenges.

Try one or more of these simple ways to bring gratitude into your world on a daily basis:

Keep a gratitude journal

You can find journals specifically made for this purpose, or simply purchase a blank journal and make it a point to write down 3-5 things you are grateful for each day. It could be as simple as, "I am grateful that I'm here to see another day" or "I am thankful to have such a beautiful home".

To mix it up, you could also give yourself a different prompt each day, such as: "I am grateful for these three... [friends / family members / objects in my home / recent experiences]", and so on.

Create a gratitude jar

Find a beautiful jar and make it a point to add small notes daily or weekly of things you are grateful for. You'll have a quick visual of all that you are grateful for every time you see it. When you are feeling down, pull out a handful of notes and read through them for an instant pick-me-up.

Tell your friends and loved ones often how thankful you are for them

Extra credit: Tell them *why* you are so thankful for them. Extra *extra* credit: Write a letter to a friend - an old-school, handwritten letter - telling them how much they mean to you. Do it at random and without expectation of anything in return.

Make it a point to compliment others

Give someone an unsolicited compliment. Bonus points if it's about something less superficial than their physical appearance or new shoes, such as the great job they are doing at work or how happy they look. Having said that, I personally enjoy compliments on a great hair day, so compliment as you see fit or as the situation calls for.

Incorporate gratitude into your meditation practice

As you settle in to meditate, concentrate on all of the things you feel grateful for in your life. First thing in the morning before getting out of bed is a great time to do this, as it will help set an awesome tone for the day.

If you want to go deeper with this practice, check out Byron Katie's, "The Work", which challenges you to look at everything in your life - the good *and* the bad - from a place of gratitude. Even the really tough stuff. This may prove to be a difficult task on some things, yes, but a willingness to look at the lessons and life decisions that even the "worst" situations have produced can help to shift your energy regarding certain people, places, and events.

Recap

How to Bring More Gratitude Into Your World

- Start a gratitude journal
- Create a gratitude jar
- Send a loved one a note about how thankful you are them
- Give someone a compliment
- Incorporate gratitude statements into your meditation practice
- Check out "The Work," by Byron Katie

Challenge

List 5 things you are grateful for today:

- _____
- _____
- _____
- _____
- _____

Additional Journaling

What thoughts or feelings does this chapter bring up for you?

_____

_____

_____

_____

_____

_____

_____

_____

_____

_____

_____

_____

_____

_____

_____

_____

_____

_____

_____

_____

_____

CREATE AN AMAZING
Morning Routine

> " "
> Does your morning routine move you
> effortlessly into high vibes?

No matter what happened the day before, we wake up each morning (hopefully) with a fresh, clean slate. How we spend those first moments of the morning can help us effortlessly set the tone for a high vibe day, or put us in lower energy that we will now spend all day actively working to reverse.

Are you sleeping in until the last possible second and now rushing to get to work? Do you start your day by grabbing your phone to check your email or social media feeds? If so, you could be setting yourself up for unnecessary distress. Of course, energy isn't permanent and there are many things we can do to help shift it – *but why make things harder than they have to be?*

I am one of those lucky, lucky people that gets to walk out my front door and put my toes in the sand within 1-3 minutes, depending on whether or not I catch the traffic light at the end of my street.★ My most peaceful and level-headed days begin with a walk on the beach. During that time, I mentally work through

65

what I have coming up for the day, what I'm most excited about, and what I'm grateful for. I'll often end my walk by sitting on the beach to do a short guided meditation, or just watch and listen to the waves crash for a few minutes.

Now, that is probably not helpful and perhaps highly irritating for those who would love to start their mornings in such a way, but are geographically unable to do so.

Edit: Since writing this book, I've moved to Montana, so I'm right there with you!

Luckily, there are plenty of things you can do to create an amazing, high-vibe morning routine, wherever you are:

Don't start your day on your phone

Consider placing your phone across the room instead of on your nightstand, forcing you to physically get out of bed in order to turn off your alarm. This can remove the temptation to lay in bed for an extra 20 minutes checking the news, email or social media - both before sleep *and* upon waking.

Take in a hit of nature first thing

Get outside if you can for some sun, or at the very least, a bit of nature to reset your mind and help to ground your energy. Weather permitting, go for a walk to process what you have coming up for the day. You could even listen to a guided meditation on your phone to create mindfulness before you get too deep into your daily tasks. Weather not cooperating with heading outdoors? Create a cozy morning spot near a window, allowing you to soak in some nature from the comfort of indoors.

Begin a gratitude practice

As mentioned earlier, it is practically *impossible* to simultaneously feel gratitude and despair. A morning gratitude practice is an awesome way to kickstart a day of positive energy. Head outside on your patio or to a sunny spot in your home with your gratitude journal and a cup of hot tea or coffee, and jot down 3-5 things you are grateful for. This time of reflection can make a huge difference in how you interact with people and the world around you as the day unfolds.

Sweat it out

If you are one of those lucky people that has an extended amount of time in the morning before other people need you, getting a morning workout in can set an awesome tone for the day. For me, a morning workout isn't just about exercise or endorphins. It also gives me a checkbox for one of my most important daily to-do's. Being able to check off that cornerstone activity early in the day gives me the confidence and momentum to tackle even more.

... *Sex* it out?

Connecting with your partner (or yourself) first thing in the morning is a great way to relieve stress, boost your mood, and improve brain cognition. Whether that takes the form of sex or snuggling is up to you – both can provide a boost to your overall vibration. Yup.

Recap

Setting Yourself Up for a Great Day

- Don't start your day on your phone
- Get out in nature first thing in the AM
- Begin a gratitude practice
- Sweat it out
- Cuddle up with someone you love

Challenge

What would a high-vibe morning look like for you?

_____

_____

_____

_____

_____

_____

_____

Now, commit to giving it a try tomorrow morning!

Additional Journaling

What thoughts or feelings does this chapter bring up for you?

_____

_____

_____

_____

_____

_____

_____

_____

_____

_____

_____

_____

_____

_____

_____

_____

_____

_____

_____

_____

_____

GET COMFORTABLE SETTING & MAINTAINING *Boundaries*

> 66
> It's time to get really comfortable
> saying "No".

One of the most important things we can do as empaths is establish and maintain clear boundaries with others. Because we do feel others' emotions very easily, it's natural for us to want to help people when they're hurting or are in need of an assist.

It's also in our nature to be concerned about, or at least acutely aware of, the comfort of those around us. This can often result in taking on things that we might not truly want to do, but feel as though we are needed for or called to do. What we do out of kindness and a pure heart can also become draining if we're not careful.

I'm not suggesting that you stop helping others, but it's important to closely monitor if and when it actually becomes a burden or drain on your own energy. Much like the airline edict to put an oxygen mask on yourself before your child in the event of an emergency, it is imperative that your own energy be high before freely giving it away to others. Otherwise, you risk deteriorating your own vibration, and your states of physical, emotional and mental health.

Not sure how to set healthy boundaries? Try the following:

Get comfortable saying "No"

If you don't feel like doing something, that is reason enough to say "no". Don't want to meet your coworkers out for drinks? Feel like twice a month is enough time to spend with your neighbors? Don't want a second date with your latest dating app match? It's perfectly ok to decline. Saying "yes" to these things may feel like the kind thing to do, but if you're going to hold resentment or annoyance over it, you're ultimately not doing anyone any favors.

When you receive an invitation to do something or to help someone, ask yourself:

- Is this something I want to do?

- Is this something I have time to do?

If you answered no to either:

- Is there something I could change about the request or invitation that would make it a more comfortable "yes" for me?

Constantly helping others with repetitive tasks? Show them how to help themselves

Always handling a task for a friend or coworker because it's "faster and easier to do it yourself" than taking the time to teach them? The next time you find yourself in that situation, take those few extra minutes to show them how you complete the task. You'll not only spare yourself time in the future, but they will also now feel empowered to handle it on their own. Win-win.

Link people with additional resources to help them with their situation

Have a friend who is always in need of a loan, or perhaps advice that borders on formal therapy sessions? Instead of being that go-to person for them, you could link them with resources that empower them to handle their situation.

In the case of a personal loan, perhaps you could express your concern and provide them with a referral for a financial budget planner. While you may feel inclined to help, it's not your responsibility to carry their load and you should not feel obligated to help unless you truly want and are able to help. This goes for any request that you don't feel you have the time or energy to tackle on their behalf.

Clarify your non-negotiables when it comes to your time

The act of saying "no" can be helped along if you have clearly defined for yourself what you need in your day or week in order to fully nurture yourself and your quality of life.

Is a daily morning workout a must? Need at least three nights a week to yourself at home? Want to put $500 a week into savings? Defining and maintaining your non-negotiables can put you in a more powerful stance for saying "yes" or "no" to others, knowing that you will not be sacrificing your basic needs and wants.

If others' feelings get hurt by your boundaries, be conscious of not letting that affect you. Adamantly maintaining your boundaries is only going to offend those who have grown accustomed to crossing them.

Recap

How to Set Healthy Boundaries

- Get comfortable saying "No"
- Show others how to help themselves
- Link people to other resources
- Clarify your non-negotiables when it comes to your time

Challenge

Identifying Your Non-Negotiables

What must you have in order to feel your best? Consider your needs with regards to your time, relationships, home, work, and finances.

_____

_____

_____

_____

_____

_____

_____

_____

_____

_____

_____

_____

_____

_____

_____

_____

_____

Additional Journaling

What thoughts or feelings does this chapter bring up for you?

_____

_____

_____

_____

_____

_____

_____

_____

_____

_____

_____

_____

_____

_____

_____

_____

_____

_____

_____

CLEAR THE
Clutter

> ❝
> Your physical space is often a direct
> reflection of your state of mind (and
> vice-versa).

One of the quickest ways to clear your mind and energy is to declutter your physical space. The appearance of your physical surroundings is a direct reflection of your life and state of mind. One could argue, "I'm busy. That's why my home is a mess right now." The reality is that chaos in our home environment can also reflect, or at least encourage, chaos in our thoughts.

Working with the Law of Attraction, it stands to reason that keeping our space clean, flowy, and peaceful would bring the same to our life and headspace. A clean and decluttered space also creates a physical and figurative blank slate for creating new things.

Maintaining a clean home is also an act of self love. You deserve to be in a beautiful, peaceful space. Always. Nurture your soul and energy with a place that feels amazing to be in.

The messiest times in my life have also been those times where I have been the most out of control. As a child - dealing with loneliness, self-doubt, and low confidence - my bedroom was a pit. I was in my room most of the time, alone. On a practical level, my room should have been incredibly neat and tidy, as I was always in it! On an emotional level, that just wasn't something that was going to happen for me. My space was a direct reflection of my state of mind and sense of self.

I can remember in the workplace, at 25-ish years old, having piles of paper on my desk to "get to later". Wanna know a secret? Later never came. Once the piles became too overwhelming, I would simply move them to another table or chair as a new pile emerged on my desk. It's no wonder I couldn't concentrate long enough to get anything done!

If you aren't naturally inclined to keep a tidy home or workspace, here are a few easy ways to tackle the decluttering process that won't leave you feeling overwhelmed:

Plan a morning or evening cleaning ritual

Not a big cleaner? Committing to a few cornerstone cleaning activities each morning and evening can go a long way in creating a feel-good home. At a basic level, putting all dishes away, picking up any clothes off the floor of your bedroom and bathroom, and wiping down your kitchen countertops can instantly make your space feel lighter.

Similarly, committing to making your bed in the morning and tidying up the kitchen after breakfast can provide the same relief and feeling of a clean space when you return home in the evening.

Set a timer and go to town

Make cleaning a fun challenge by setting a timer for 3-5 minutes and get busy cleaning one space in your home. In the kitchen, 3-5 minutes might get you clean countertops, dirty dishes put away, and a swept floor. Trust me, you will move faster than usual if there's a timer egging you on.

If you have multiple people living in your home, lucky you. Let everyone pick their own space to clean, and see how far a few minutes can collectively get you.

On a decluttering / purge mission? Tackle just one drawer, shelf, or cabinet at a time

When we get on a mission to declutter, it's natural to get overzealous and remove EVERYTHING from a space at once. Now you're two hours in, you're over it, and you have essentially just moved your mess from your closet to the floor of your bedroom. Instead, pick one shelf or drawer at a time to tackle. Once complete, you may feel energized to organize another one. And if not, that's ok - you at least haven't created a *new* mess.

There's an opposite end of the spectrum to consider in all of this as well. Some people clean to the point of obsession, perhaps to distract themselves or because *any* sign of clutter is too overwhelming for their mind. And again, I would say that yes, our space is a reflection of what's going on inside of us. Perhaps you could try to work on relaxing your standards for yourself and the cleanliness of your home.

At the end of the day, simply assess what impact your home is having on you and what you may want to change in order to release that impact. As with every challenge in this book, I recommend creating a plan that feels light and manageable for you.

Recap

Simple Ways to Declutter Your Space

- Plan a morning or evening cleaning ritual
- Set a timer to tackle individual tasks or areas of your home
- Tackle just one drawer, shelf, or cabinet at a time

Challenge

Create a Decluttering Ritual

Try these simple routines to keep clutter at bay:

AM
- Make bed
- Clean breakfast dishes
- Pick clothes/towels up from floor

PM
- Wash dishes
- Wipe down kitchen countertops

Once/Weekly
- Sweep/vacuum
- Deep clean bathrooms
- Dust entire home
- Sort through mail

Additional Journaling

What thoughts or feelings does this chapter bring up for you?

_____

_____

_____

_____

_____

_____

_____

_____

_____

_____

_____

_____

_____

_____

_____

_____

_____

_____

_____

_____

_____

WORK IT *Out*

> **"**
> We hold our issues in our tissues

If you're a fan of massages, you've likely been told by a massage therapist that you "hold your issues in your tissues." Our bodies hold onto all manners of toxins we take in, from negative thoughts and energy to low quality foods, alcohol, and beyond. Whatever the source, it can sit in your system and bog down both your energy and mood.

One of the quickest ways to release this is to literally sweat it out. That process can take many forms, from going for a run, lifting weights at the gym, sitting in a sauna, or taking a hot bath. Sweat can carry out some of that toxicity from your system, leaving your vibration and mood a little lighter.

Some quick ways to sweat it out:

Get in a cardio workout

Choose a speed and intensity that gets you sweating the fastest. For me, an outdoor run, no matter the season or weather, leaves me looking like I've just taken a shower. Can't maintain a top speed for an extended period of time? Try alternating quick bursts of speed with a minute or so of walking. You'll get the boost in heart rate that gets you sweating, without exhausting yourself. You'll also get the added benefit of feel-good endorphins.

Hop in a sauna or steam room

Infrared saunas are particularly awesome, as they more directly heat your body versus the air, allowing you to experience a more intense sweat at a lower temperature. You can even purchase an infrared sauna blanket for at-home use.

Take a hot bath

Add some Epsom or mineral salts to your bathwater for additional health and beauty benefits, including smoother skin, reduced soreness in your joints and muscles, and stress relief. A few drops of an essential oil can also supercharge your mood. For a boost in energy, try a refreshing oil, such as peppermint, lemon, or sweet orange. For relaxation, try lavender, rose, or chamomile.

Get a massage

Another great way to move toxins out of your cells is with massage, particularly the deep tissue variety. The key there will be to drink plenty of water afterwards to help move out the waste and toxins that are now freely flowing through your body.

You can also try self-massage techniques, such as foam rolling or trigger point therapy, to get things moving in your body.

If you've made it this far into the book, you're probably seeing where you can double and triple down on your vibration-raising activities. An outdoor run, first thing in the morning, in the sunshine can knock out three vibe-lifting activities in one fell swoop.

Recap

Simple Ways to Sweat It Out

- Hit the gym
- Sit in a sauna or steam room
- Take a hot bath with Epsom salts
- Treat yourself to a massage

Challenge

Work It Out

Commit to getting in one or more of these activities at least 3 times this week!

- Cardio or strength training workout
- Sauna or steam session
- Hot bath
- Massage

Additional Journaling

What thoughts or feelings does this chapter bring up for you?

_____

_____

_____

_____

_____

_____

_____

_____

_____

_____

_____

_____

_____

_____

_____

_____

_____

_____

_____

_____

BONUS: PRACTICE THE
Art of Surrender

> ❝
> The need to know is ultimately a fear-based practice. And the Universe most powerfully responds to faith, not fear.

Letting go is probably one of the most powerful things you can do to keep your vibration high. Releasing the need to control a situation can create immediate peace of mind. What may feel like a terrible situation now could reveal itself as a blessing a day from now, a week from now, or perhaps *years* from now.

And maybe it doesn't. But "needing to know" is ultimately a fear-based practice. If you believe in the Law of Attraction, then you have an understanding that when you live in a fear-based reality, you simply usher in… more things to be afraid of.

The Universe most powerfully responds to faith, not fear.

If you are relying on external energy tools - tarot cards, mediums or spiritual healers - to provide you with all of the "answers", you might ultimately be blocking what's meant for you by sending out an overload of demanding, fear-based energy. I am personally friends with several energy healers, and what I usually find is that the guidance they provide me is simply validation of what I was already intuiting.

When we are constantly looking to others for answers, by spiritual means or otherwise, we are ultimately giving away our power. How many times have you, in trying to make a decision, asked multiple friends, family members, and business associates for their advice? Subconsciously, we're looking either for validation of what we already know we want to do or validation that what we're too afraid to do is, in fact, not the best idea. Validation works both ways, positively and negatively.

As empaths, we do naturally pick up on things, which you surely know by now is both a blessing and a curse. It's important to place our trust in our own intuition over "higher" knowledge from others.

Having said that, it can be good to check in from time to time with someone that you consider a little more awakened or experienced than you, to help direct you on your path. Much like any other teacher, they can show you new ways to use your intuition to hear that higher guidance for yourself. But please don't forget that at some point, we will outgrow our teachers. Be conscious of who and where you turn to for guidance and advice.

While it could be helpful to ask for more insights or alternative viewpoints that show you the full picture of a situation, try to refrain from demanding the answer. The answers can only come from you. Could that result in a "disaster" or undesired outcome? Sure - but it was your outcome to have and no one else's. Whatever you decide, there is a purpose and a lesson that is all yours for the taking.

IN CLOSING

The ability to pick up on the energy around us is an enormous blessing, and one that should not be taken lightly. Hold space and gratitude for this gift, and all that it allows you to create and do in your life, work, and relationships.

Want to dive deeper in living your highest vibe life?

Visit me at www.JustOneWoo.com

RESOURCES

JUST
ONE WOO

Additional Energy Management Tools

Visit www.JustOneWoo.com/EmpathDetox to access the tools mentioned in this book, including:

- Binaural Beats Playlists
- Social Media Aggregator Apps
- High-Vibe Music Playlists

EMPATHS.*biz*

Coaching for empathic and heart-centered entrepreneurs:

Work looks and feels different when you're a highly-sensitive empath. I'm fiercely passionate about helping my fellow empathic + heart-centered souls thrive in both business and life. Abundance and mission can happily co-exist!

Classic empath behavior has many of us:

- Severely devaluing our time and services
- Suffering from imposter syndrome or perfectionism
- Feeling constant overwhelm and stress
- Always putting others' needs before our own
- Having a hard time saying 'no'
- Giving too much of ourselves without reciprocity

It's not our fault. So much of this has to do with the energies we absorb around us, as well as coping mechanisms we developed in childhood. No more. We deserve to feel amazing in our work - and receive abundance for it!

Visit me at www.empaths.biz for:

- 1:1 Business Coaching
- Soul-Aligned Marketing Strategies
- Professional Storytelling Services
- **Content Strategy + Execution**

About The Author

Colleen Wolak
Empathic Entrepreneur,
Storyteller & Marketing Coach

Growing up, I always felt "different." It was easy to attribute my shy, anxious behaviors to being a slightly overweight kid (and extremely overweight young adult). Now, I understand that this was all part of being an empath. But at the time, I was just an observer to everyone around me, and adjusting my behavior to protect myself.

That shyness, that outside observer within me, gave me what I now consider to be one of my biggest superpowers: the ability to fully see people, and emotionally connect to their inner truth. It's a skill I've always subconsciously used in my professional marketing background, and now harness fully in my storytelling and personal coaching work.

Around the time I discovered and began to embrace my superpower, I also became more open to my spirituality and the idea that we do not have to follow the classic programming of life.

As I've entered into more spiritual circles, I still feel a little "different" at times - as though half of me resides in the 5D and the other half firmly planted in the 3D. Too "woo-woo" for my less spiritual friends, and a little too logical or earthly for my more spiritual friends. Yet I feel equally drawn to and comfortable in both circles. Afterall, we are all spiritual beings, sharing together in this human experience.

I'm passionate about bridging the gap between the classic programming of our 3D life and the dreaminess of our 5D spirituality. I very much live in the "gray" and love helping others do the same.

But please don't call me "woo-woo".... *just one woo here!*

I know there are many others like me, constantly working to navigate that beautifully gray space between 5D spirituality and 3D living.

Connect with me in this beautiful space at www.JustOneWoo.com.

Printed in the United States
by Baker & Taylor Publisher Services